Shallow Waters

Tristin Jacy

Shallow Waters

ISBN: 0692860177
ISBN-13: 978-0692860175

DEDICATION

This book is dedicated to all the hearts searching for love in all the wrong places in hopes that this will serve as a reminder to love yourself first and foremost.

ACKNOWLEDGMENTS

I am beyond grateful for those people whose love and loyalty
have encouraged and supported me not only through this
journey, but in life. I truly believe that it is who we surround
ourselves with, the circle of people we trust and the tribe we
create that helps shape our lives as well as how we learn to
see the world.

The following pages are filled with words, lessons, and
heartache. Some mine, some simply inspired by stories that
were shared and entrusted to me. Either way thanks must be
given for the lessons life has provided, and yes even for the
heartache - for without it these words would have never
found their way onto the page. So a sincere thanks is given to
those who trusted me with their stories and their feelings and
of course to the men who I loved, tried to love
and left in love.
Without you my heart would not be as full as it is.

At this time I must gratefully and lovingly acknowledge my
children, Aiyana and Khayri who give me breath, and inspire
me to be the best version of myself. They are who have truly
taught me the meaning of love. To my mother, because she
is responsible for my endless love of books and poetry. She
was the first to introduce me to the power of words,
storytelling and who ultimately gave me the inspiration to
create

Throughout my life there have been so many people who have both inspired and encouraged me to write. My gratitude to all those who have taught me or been the source of that inspiration is endless. I would however, like to first thank those who were directly instrumental in the creation of this book: Erica Peterman, Chasity Drumgoole-Omotoyo, Hassan El Saddique, James Ponzo & Shelly Inniss-Jackson, over the years, I can recall countless times that each of you at some point, told me that I had a story to tell and to just write. You have all taken time out to read my words scribbled on paper, or sent to you in texts at crazy hours and each time you read and responded with encouragement.

Cornelius Newman, you have always supported me, pushed me to write when I didn't want to, unknowingly inspired me, and have endured every mood and emotion I had to go through in order to complete this process.

William Palmer, you were one of the first people I ever shared my notebook with. I trusted you with my words and ever since, you have motivated me, always pushing me to finish. DJ Bionicman, thank you for helping to make that first publication possible all those years ago. You have always encouraged my dreams.

Jonie Lax, you gave countless Tuesday mornings to meet with me which kept me on track and kept me motivated. Even if we spent hours talking about everything else, other than writing, somehow it all just worked. You were there for each step, each confused effort and every draft. For that, I am forever grateful.

Also, thank you to Jason Williams, of Upstate Multimedia, for seeing my vision and making it come to life.

Family consists of those people who stand by you in the best and worst times, who love and accept you at your worst and motivate you to be your best. So with that being said, thank you to Kelly McLean, John Massey, Samari Angel, Sharif Lewis, Lindsey Taylor, Mike Davis, Maya Baxter, Wendie Norwood, Jessica & Derrick Baity, Derrick Turner, Arthur Lewis, Anthony Taylor, Dorian Reeves, Laquin Gibson, Rich Jarrett, Jason Grey Sr., Danielle Womack, Satoria Donovan, Kevin Abernathy, Robert Gray, Frederick Gilbert, Mary Topinko, Candace Davis, Sheila Krajnak, Nicole Mason, Tiffany Smallwood, Jamar Corbett, Holly Quicksey, Sandra Washington, Leasa Rochester-Mills, Florence Johnson, Darnell Salter, my cousin, Philip Gerviss, Aunt Patti and Uncle Mike, Aunt Nancy and cousin Kali, my brother Rene DeBellaistre, my nephews Mason, Elijah & Bryce & Braden. My nieces Avah & Zion, my god-daughter Aubrey Massey, and of course my 3rd Jason Grey who is forever one of my own. I also can't forget my entire Ravens and 716 United family. Thank you all so much for being my support system over these past few years. Each of you will forever be a part of me. I am thankful to be blessed by such an amazing circle of people. I have a deep sense of gratitude for *all* those who I hold close to my heart. Please believe that I value your friendship and love more than anything.

Last but not least, I must express thanks to the higher power. Even in the darkest moments I have been able to find my voice, find my way and find love because of faith; faith in an unknown voice, and an unknown power higher than myself.

With growth comes pain
A flower can't blossom without the right amount of
rain

-Tristin Jacy

PREFACE

Our relationships, both past and present, become a part of us. All the ways we grew and all the things we learned and experienced become woven intricately into the fabric of our souls, forever changing us. However much we may learn from these experiences, the relationship that we have with our self is by far the most important.

Oftentimes I hear people complain about being single, about bad dates, failed marriages, horrible break-ups and devastating heartbreaks. While we may be able to relate to their stories and understand their frustrations it is important for us not to lose ourselves in the negativity. I learned the hard way, early on, that finding love is not about completion or filling an empty void in your life. The only love that will ever heal or complete you is the love you have for yourself.

"Shallow Waters" is a poetic expression of how the wrong relationships can hold us back. If we are wading in shallow waters looking for depth we will never find ourselves. These relationships do not work because they were never meant to, they were merely meant to serve as a lesson. Be thankful for the lessons that life gives you, for this is what makes us who we are; this is what strengthens us. A relationship should never hinder your growth or constrain you in any way. When you love yourself and embrace the lessons that you learned, then you will begin to attract only what is meant for you.

Love is beautiful. Love for ourselves is absolutely necessary. Love with the right person should always help us grow, and allow us to be the best version of ourselves. Always, always believe in love.

SHADOWS OF THE MOON

Was thrown to the wolves
So I let 'em raise me
Was always thought to be wild,
but ultimately it's what made me feel free...

There's strength in vulnerability

but all you choose to see is weakness.
While I find strength in these lessons
You look past my good intentions
only
finding negativity
in my need to run free...

In a world where love is endangered
we are all territorial by nature
needing loyalty to survive.

But it was something in your eyes
I sensed what you tried so hard to hide
within all your layers of uncertainty
Nothing made sense to me
I had to break free...

Infatuated with who you thought I was
you smothered every bit of us
the more you tried to change me
the more I struggled to be free....

Recently, you said you search for a glimpse of me
in the shadows of the moon
I can't help but wonder
why you couldn't just run free
    with me

CIRCLES

North, South, East, West

Never lost, just
follow your heart they say

Tried to make the right choice
Searching for the right thing to say

A silent voice
Hold on, let go

Goodbye doesn't always feel right;
Things tend to go wrong
Even after you were so sure it was right

As if I need another reason not to sleep at night

When do you let it go?
When do you fight?

I should have just let you in
In my head, in my heart, in my life

Paying the price
For fear of what could go wrong

Never seeing what would go right
Layers upon layers to your depth

Yet so many moments empty
Trust can't be built on a foundation you forget to lay

North, South, East, West

Some days I thought we'd find our way
Somehow we got lost with the rest

Ups and downs
Smiles and frowns
We just keep going around and around

Circles

Should mean we're complete
Yet we're knee deep

In confusion
Not even holding me as we sleep

Emotions run deep
The perfect illusion

Stay, walk away
I never told you to leave
You never asked me to stay

Searching trying to find my way
With you
Without you

North, South, East, West

I can't figure you out
Walking a fence
Somehow you made sense

I wanted to walk with you
On the road less traveled
Emotions honest, unraveled

Lost, found
We just keep going around and around

North, South, East, West

Circles
Incomplete
Knee deep
In all the words we never said

METAPHOR

I like him like a metaphor
familiar, like I knew him before
Maybe in a past life, eyes that entice
Intellect with a bit of swag in his walk
Has that passion for his people when he talk
Well read; self-taught
A little like Kendrick
& a whole lotta what I like

I like him like a metaphor,
Unfamiliar, like I never knew him before
Unraveled like an unsolved mystery,
like incomplete poetry
A story left unread
Like words still unsaid
He leaves me wanting more

I like him like a metaphor
He has the words that rhyme
To the last line I wrote
He is the art to the canvas of my heart
It is as if we have loved before
In a past life
He's the left to my right

I like him like a metaphor

FYI

We live in a world where you can text,
instant message, snap chat, poke and Face Time
yet fail to value anyone's actual time!
Wasting time rather than investing in quality time!

Never realizing that tomorrow isn't promised – we are living
on borrowed time.

We listen more to respond then we do to hear
And search endlessly, looking for the right one
Rather than trying to *become*
The right one
Do you feel where I'm coming from?

Love & loyalty are words we hear but seldom see, thrown
around carelessly
Expecting to simply be handed "what's meant to be"

You want love to be easy, basically stress free,
instantaneously uploaded
But feelings have become so commercialized that when
someone is real they are thought to be fake
Because fake has become popularized
on YouTube & reality TV
Nothing can flow naturally when you can't express what you
want it to be

I believe there were so many good intentions
But then why so much distance, tension

Disagreements make it so easy to walk away...
Guess it's too much effort to stay,

Hearts are no longer worn on sleeves
Running from Cupid as if love is a disease.
Just another conspiracy.
So words from the heart, thought out,
Written rather than spoken
Become ridiculed
As unauthentic
Instead of felt

Remember when love letters were thought to be romantic?
Now we analyze the subtext of a text
And forget the simplicity of the moment when our hands
first met

From the first kiss, walls were built
Perhaps thought to protect but all it did was divide
You pulled away, in that last kiss
Words analyzed

Words...
Written or spoken
Words, formed from the heart
Struggling to understand the mind

We can't learn from our mistakes until we admit
That our biggest issue with communication
Is the illusion
That it ever really took place.

BLAMED IT ON LOVE

I let my words bleed on to the page;
Exposed
The words were there for him to read
Yet the book remained closed
I tried to tell my story
Feeling like the ending was written all along
No matter how I wrote it
He always read me wrong

Never seeing my scars as strength
it was as if he questioned my independence
& was never clear in his intentions
as if choices don't have consequence
so after some time he simply lost my attention

he claimed I disregarded his values
simply because I didn't need him to come to my rescue
I had learned long ago that
You'll never find depth when the water is shallow

And these so called values changed to suit his argument
to cover up his confusion
{a victim of false enlightenment}

too busy dissecting others to ever look in the mirror
the failure to see how strength comes from fear &
vulnerability
the damage it did was permanent
gave him chance after chance
Forgiveness without apology

And still…
He *never* saw what I could see:
He had scars from a broken heart
pain of a soul once torn apart
the resistance to feel anything; *something*

Ultimately, he had become *all* of what had hurt him
and blamed it on love.

OUR DYSFUNCTIONAL LOVE AFFAIR

Intensity
Pulls me in
A fire beneath my skin
Lust
Throbbing
Kissing my chin
My neck
Until lips meet
Fantasies whispered between the sheets
Your body speaks to me
Craving you
To do what you do
Intoxicating
Seduction
Every time our eyes meet
Every time our lips and body meet
Undress me
Kissing my skin
Deep within
Hold me, lift me
Pleasure
Extreme
Take me where I want to be
Awaken me
At first glance I had a prediction
As if I already knew you
My desire; *my addiction*

CONFUSION

Too in tune with ourselves to give in to one another
Surrendering completely, not to each other

Well read, well spoken, well versed
Souls immersed

In higher knowledge, a higher consciousness
Simplicity and complexity
Intellect and creativity

Layers to the soul
With the intent to keep our minds open
But still our hearts were protected
Searching for a connection

Needing reassurance
Yet needing no one

Or so we believed

Messages received
Literally, figuratively
Left to read between the lines
At times -
Messages subliminal

Unable to put their hearts on the line
But connected in time and space

Searching for that safe place
Finding it between pillows and sheets

Conversations inspired by wine
Losing track of time
Perfection
Reading the energy yet still walking this fine line
Were you ever really mine?

You left a piece of yourself
In return I told you how I felt
Words written, silence spoken
A heart broken

Feelings once intertwined
Finding each other, only at times
Passion drained from overthinking
We complicated what should have been so simple

Losing ourselves in our own thoughts
Creating doubts where there were none

There was nothing forced about you finding
Your way inside me, naturally
Nothing forced in you asking me to stay

I wanted all the parts of you
Your mind, your heart
We simply got in our own way
There was so much I wanted to say

We aren't all we are supposed to be
Nor are we all we could be

Simple, inconvenient honesty
We may not want to see
But need to see
How is that for a logical fallacy?

Distorted positions
Because *WE* couldn't listen
To words that were never said

Perhaps you should have spoken
My words were there for you to have read
I can't get inside your head
to hear
    all the things you never said

Is it too late to find our way?
    Back
Two minds, two hearts, two souls
Too bright, too smart
Too scared

PERCEPTION IS REALITY

Loyalty is so often out of convenience
expected yet not always reciprocated
Truth, in moments, perhaps at times...
Convince me
Authenticity even exists

Perception alters reality
    Becomes reality
    Changes reality

A victim of your insecurity
Assumptions and scrutiny
Seems like it's the one who points their finger who always
turns out to be guilty

Blood is thicker than water
And yet you need water to survive
When will we realize
Those closest often have the most to hide
The ultimate mistrust

Taken more than they give
Superficial motives
Seldom forgive
Twisted irony
Sense of entitlement
With needs never met
Never satisfied

Those lacking empathy
With their self-centered stories
Always focused on "me"
Eyes wide shut
Yet still passing judgement

Perception alters reality
    Becomes reality
    Changes reality

Convince me,
In the ability
Convince me,
Of your authenticity;
Consistency.

    Convince me.

IF THIS IS A GAME

What keeps you coming back?

    Love or lust
Silence isn't honest
Mixed messages
Rejection

Here then gone
Too much room for assumption

Often incorrect

Tell me what to expect
Good intentions
What about actions
Saying nothing says a lot

Doors open

{Hearts closed}
    No response
Repeating what we never repaired

Wanting it, but too scared
Attached yet unattached

Wants, needs
Fear intercedes
    Interrupts

Desire crept in
Under our skin
Bodies intertwined
    Ecstasy
      Time after time

What are you trying to tell me

When you reach out
After pushing me away
Days long, nights longer
Heart beating stronger

Don't know the rules, if this is a game
    What do we gain?

LOVE ME, DESPITE

Sometimes you run out of tears
Lost in shadows
Suffocated by fears

You can't understand
    Pain

    So deep

Nightmares still haunt even the most peaceful nights of sleep

    Torn
    Broken
    Empty
    Numb

The past is what made me
Broke me and built me

Innocence stolen
    Love died
    Life taken

How much can these shoulders take
Found the strength to survive
Having to stand alone

Heal
Kneel
Pray

A heart in pieces still open for love
Kiss the pain away
Love me despite these broken pieces
Love me despite the shadows that linger
Love me enough to
    Stay

FOREVER IS A LIE

Changed, crashed, burned
One moment, one decision
Lessons unlearned
Silence
For too long
Changes everything.
Leaving us with nothing,
When you had nothing to say
Counting days
You didn't have the time
But really you had nothing but time
Choices
Forging a new reality
All we built shattered
Love, another fatality
Left empty
I walked away
Years lost in a day
Still claiming you tried
Tears that never fell
Unable to cry
It's hard to even listen
Guess you thought there was never a me, without you

If forever is a lie, can love ever be true?

SO MUCH, SO LITTLE

It matters so much
It matters so little

Days, months, years; time apart
Pieces of a broken heart

Will we ever find our way
What is left to say?

Perhaps love is a misconception
Loyalty merely a conversation

After all this time
We realize forever's a lie

Answers disguised
Desire will arise

Getting lost in your eyes
The moment your lips touch mine

When you reach for my hand
Suddenly you'll understand

I was always yours, you were always mine

Time changes nothing
　　Everything

Two souls, one heart
Beating
Together, apart

It means so much
It means so little

When you say you love me
　　Words
Then put nothing above me
　　Actions

Simple
Yet so complicated

Will we make it?

You say so much
You say so little

Feelings disguised in silence
Can't help but wonder what was meant

You have proved so much
You have proved so little
Can I trust you
Have you actually given me reason not to?

We've grown so much
We've grown so little

Part of you
Part of me

Hearts in need
We've loved so much
We've loved so little

I need you
You need me

We need so much
We need so little

Have we found our way?

It matters so much
It matters so little

The question is, do I even want to stay?

SMALL TALK

Talk to me, call me, learn me
Intrinsically

Dreading the repetitive "hey what's up" texts
As if you're struggling to come up with what to say next

Eluding small talk; give me something deep
Spare me your voice virtually on repeat
Peel back the layers,
Give me that conversation that'll last hours
Let me see you
Paint me a picture

Question me, challenge me, teach me
Disagree

Anything but the typical Q & A
Avoid the cliché

I crave deep thoughts
Natural; unrefined
When it comes easy; never forced
Completely immersed

{Good conversation is *so* hard to find}

REAL OR CONTRIVED

No answer, no reply
One word
Late response, no response
Why try
You give what you get
But how much of yourself did you ever really give?
Leave, come back
Forget, forgive

When did we ever really try?

Pointing fingers at me
All out of apologies
You avoided any real conversation
Rejection
Little to no effort
You can't settle
So then am I supposed to settle?
Unable to break down your wall
Unable to feel your heart
No answer, no reply
Frustration
Questioning why
Connection
Real or contrived
Searching your eyes
For the missing piece
Will you ever realize?

HEART FAILURE

My heart
    Abused
    Broken
    Taken for granted
Once, you even said it was damaged

Sometimes I try and wonder what I'm trying for
I'd fight, but what am I fighting for?

My heart is tired
Tired of being misled
    Mistreated
It's barely beating

Picturing you leaving
No understanding
My love
My needs
No I never wore it on my sleeve

Never captured the butterflies
Nor recited poetry
That lay captive needing to breathe
My heart
    Alone

In the depths of all that's dark
Thought you had awakened me
But the joke was on me

Moments empty
My heart empty

Craving passion
Depth, endless love
A kiss, fingers intertwined

A sign
Anything
To let me know I was still alive

I needed to feel

The beat of your drum
The beat of my heart

I needed to feel

Words that ran deep
Simplicity woven in meaning

Raw honesty
Needed to feel
Your complexity

On top of me
Within me

My heart
Misled
Mistreated
Misunderstood
Broken, misused

Yet
It STILL beats

SUGAR AND SPICE
And all Things Nice

"Sugar & Spice
And all things nice
That is what little girls are made of…"

Perfect, pretty and virtuous
Expectations, fabrications
Willing to pay the price to be the perfect wife
A fairytale of sweet perfection
Shattered because it was ALL an illusion

Fighting thoughts, a heart's intrusion
Unwoven, shattered misconceptions

I need raw honesty, no deception
Like the *"Rose that Grew from Concrete"*
When the possible and the impossible meet

Love, come on now, open your eyes-
I'm NOT gentle and sweet
Soft spoken or weak

My words can be calculated, precise
And at times they can slice
Right through your ego
    But then again,
perhaps they will change your life
Turn wrongs into rights
Days into nights

Kisses that ignite, the words I've chosen to write
Even between these sweet words, orchestrated
My feelings narrated
You'll never catch my heart on my sleeve,
These thoughts often hard to read

You'll never hear me say it's *you* I need
Because
What I NEED is to breathe, to live
And love, to run free knowing you're beside me
Loyalty

Don't try to change me, complete me
I don't need you to rescue me
I am NOT broken, nor am I lost

Never leave words unspoken
Or leave me guessing,
My mind is open for you to explore, inspire, seduce
with the complexity of your intellect

Thoughts intertwine, connecting us
And at times, maybe even separating us

I won't always agree, or see it your way
There will be days that aren't easy

And in my stubbornness know I may make it worse
I may not be quick to apologize
I may not let you see the tears in my eyes,
Most likely I'll disguise my vulnerability

It may take you an eternity to peel back the layers, of
        my heart, my past, my soul
But know it's with you I'm trying to grow, beside you, right
before you

My love is not perfect
It was not tailor made for you
Yet I humbly offer it to you

It may not always
be well written, or well spoken
But it is real, it is loyal, it is everything

For you, I would lay my pride aside
For you, I would try
For it's you, I'm trying to let inside

Provided, you meet me half way
Proving your intent to stay

So *no*, I'm not all things nice
A little sugar but a whole lot of spice

Distance and connectedness
Confusion and understanding
Reality with a hint of allusion
Poetry written yet never recited
I may not be all that you dreamed
or wanted, *but* I'll be all that you need

2 AM

It's 2 am and I'm scribbling words you'll probably never read
Clock strikes three
& I just want you here with me
But even when you're here
You're not always here
Present, yet mind so far away
Complicated irony
Twisted fallacy
Your heart simply won't trust me
Treating love like the enemy
My patience is drained
These puzzle pieces
arranged
Methodically, perfectly
Fitting one into the other
Just as you fit into me
Estranged
You threw the pieces to the floor
I can't take any more
Feelings ignored, no remorse
unapologetic
Pain, frustration

Somehow so poetic

MY REFLECTION
A LOVE LETTER TO MYSELF

Hiding behind walls
A mind forged penitentiary
    An introvert
Fearful of exposing what hurts

Eyes flirt tempting to divert
Any and all reality
    Can't share
    Won't share
Heart unaware

Blinded by the glare
of your own reflection
As you avoid rejection, you limit your conversation
Actions guided by YOUR own hesitation

As much as you hide, *I can see right through you*
Transparently masked
Hard for you to grasp
How *I* can see what you try so hard to hide

I recognize the loneliness and pain
I understand your need to refrain
Scared to make the same mistakes
Even when it's real you still see it as fake

Perhaps *I* relate
Your words, your actions *I* can explicate
Because *I've* once written them, lived them

The metaphorical connections
Are no coincidence
The feeling you get as you look at the new moon
Is the reason we are always in tune
You see me as a mirror
To all that you desire, all that you fear

You hear the words *I* can't say
Feel the pain *I* thought *I* had tucked away
Can't hide what another will recognize
Why not embrace the darkness
Nothing is as peaceful as the night's sky

Do not forsake me because *I* can see beauty in your
imperfections
With you *I* can bare my flaws
My secrets
Those dark moments that
You are afraid to let anyone see
Yet you chose to give them to *me*
And you ran rather than facing reality
Rather be alone than bare your soul to *me*

Insecurities
Hard to admit our similarities
Where there's strength there's weakness
Reciprocity

Life wasted, hearts jaded
To avoid undressing and leaving our souls naked
All too complicated when honesty and transparency are
options
Over inconsistency

Like poetry there is beauty in pain
It all pertains
Look deep within your soul, whether you know it or not, it's
already exposed

In the light of the moon, stare at your refection
Learn to see yourself as *I* see you
Battle scars and bruises
However intrusive

Imperfections beautifully woven together
One day *I* hope you
Let someone love you as *I* love you
As time won't last forever

DESIRE

Thoughts

Consume me
Overwhelm me
Drawn to you
Wanting you
Desire
Lust
Craving you
A kiss on the neck
Till there's nothing left
Of your imagination
Infatuation
Wrap yourself in me
Arms around me
Passion
Seduction
Everything I need to know is in your kiss
Your lips
On the small of my back
A connection
Intense
Addicted
To the high you give

UNEXPECTED

We started exploring each other's body
and got lost in one another's mind
Creating a love; a life - not presumed at the time

A perfect love affair; unexpected
From the time we first met
An instant connection

Craving his presence
Passionate sex

Loved watching him walk
With his bow legged ass
Sexually a perfect match

That look in his eyes
All the things it implied
He made love to my mind
Undressed my soul

Fantasies whispered between the sheets
Feelings now indiscreet

Attraction; desire
Love inspired

He found his way in; got under my skin
The story begins where we thought it might end

All of him
All of me
I'm a part of him; he's a part of me

Lust grew vehemently
Heart's now connected indefinitely.

LOVE RE-WRITTEN

If we could go back to that chilly, Saturday afternoon
When our eyes first met,
An attraction all too soon

If we could simply go back to a time
Before you lied
Before our hands, lives and hearts intertwined
If we could just take our time
    Simply rewind

A complicated mess from the start
It's no surprise we are left with broken hearts
Desire consumed us
Drowned us
And several times it even saved us

That magnetic draw always bringing me back to you
Back to the chaos, back in your arms
Never questioned if you loved me, wanted me
you may have even needed me

But I always read between the lines
Caught you in all your countless lies

And the more I pulled away
the more you would convince me to stay

The desire that filled up in those soft brown eyes
The way your hand would graze my thighs

      I couldn't resist
Addicted to the lust, addicted to the sex
Filling me with pleasure, but leaving me so empty

If we could go back… could we re-write our story
Edit our mistakes, make some revisions
Could we create a new life if it were all re-written?

LIE AFTER LIE

Year after year, lie after lie, you always
Made me believe the shit was all in my mind

You knew I wasn't the type to go snoopin' around tryin' to
prove shit
So you kept telling me I was makin' up problems that didn't
exist

You'd turn the tables and find something wrong;
Crazy how a man will make you feel guilty for something he's
done

'Trust me' – you said
'Just love me' – you said

So I gave you chance after chance,
Somedays it felt like I was losing my damn mind
But I didn't wanna give up when I had given you so much of
my time

You would always seduce and comfort me with lies
Lied so much you lost sight of the truth

And to think of all the things you accused me of…

Lowered my expectations to be with you
    A harsh reality even I didn't want to believe was true

Guess at that point I was living a lie anyway
Every time you kissed me, you'd kiss away my doubts
Every time I tried to walk away you said you couldn't stand
the thought
Always checking on my whereabouts

The more I'd try and pull away the more you would convince
me to stay

I loved you but I hated you

I don't even think you cared; long as I didn't leave your ass
When I'd get mad you would simply laugh talkin' 'bout how
cute it was

Everything you did that I would feel was suspicious
You'd convince me I was just trippin'; it was all in my head

Trust me' – you said
Just love me'- you said

THEN here she comes all upset… sayin' you were *hers*

…you know what?
SHE CAN HAVE YOUR ASS
Losing me is exactly what you deserve.

HER

So I've heard you were talking shit
All this nonsense & *'dust to side chicks'*
How about you're way outta context
Convincing yourself *I'm* somehow the enemy
Guess based on who you were talking to
You *wanted* it to get back to me

Like him, all you wanted was to
ease your own insecurities

Anyhow, I understand all this speculation got you mad
But what's funny is you're not *actually* mad at him;
only me?
Well how's that for instability?

If after all his wrongs, you *STILL* wanna claim him
Then I think it's safe to say that
You can stop comin' for me;
After all,
if he's really yours, shouldn't you demand some loyalty
Instead you're too busy running your mouth, slandering
me.

*Wish you'd give as much thought to your own worth as you
do worrying about me.*

He lied to me; just like he lied to you
He claims to love me;
just like I'm sure he claims to love you too
He hurt me; just like he hurt you

Even after I caught him with you
He's STILL lying, refusing to claim you
He was texting me while he was sitting right next to you

I gave you the truth, if nothing else
And yet you continue to play yourself
Guess you just want someone else to blame
'cause you still got somethin' to say every time
you hear my name
& you don't have anything else to do but
stalk my social media page?
Come on now, I'm gonna need you to act your age!

It's like you keep looking for an apology
But it ain't gonna come from me
Why do you think I'm the one who owes you?
I already told you; *HE* is the one you need to look to

If anything, I owe myself an apology
And maybe, just maybe…
You owe yourself more than *this* too.

THE BREAK UP

Never thought you could make me cry
'I love you', being my favorite
of all your lies

Can't find the words
Can't find a way
Had to leave
But wanted to stay

All that I gave you
Times I forgave you

Still, all I can think of is you

Can barely breathe
The emptiness is killing me
keep expecting you to text me

My dysfunction
My downfall
...my balance,
my calm

A perfect seduction
Everything I want
Everything I need
My harsh reality

Too many nights alone
Too many things unknown
Too many times I couldn't decipher
Between the truth and the lies

You always claimed that everything you said,
    you did actually mean
how was I supposed to know which parts to believe

Never thought you could make me cry
'I love you', being my favorite
of all of your lies

STILL A PART OF ME

The truth was too hard to face
Had me feeling like I needed space
walked out that night
hoping you'd follow me
hoping you thought it was worth the fight
You said you weren't gonna respond just to make me feel
right

I never wanted to be so wrong in my life

We've always been complicated
under one another's skin; I just can't explain it
a symptom of withdrawal
a gamble; risking it all
lust, love
everything wrong, but it felt so right
I always came back to you; and you knew I would
    They told me not to trust you
    warned me not to fall for you
took my chances cause in life there's no guarantee
surprised them all when I fell
               & you caught me

I became a part of you, and you a part of me

Six year love affair, each night hotter than the last
Two dark pasts makin' the future look bright

Encourage me, lift me up
We'd fight just to make up,
Never tried to change me, never tried to change you
Loved you right, loved you wrong
I made you weak, you made me strong
It was nothin' but love all along

And yet here we are,
So close but so far
Layin in this bed, but you're not here
Fighting the tears, 'cause what's the point

Never wanted to be so wrong in my life

A PAINFUL END

Never underestimate a man's power to make you feel guilty
for their mistakes
to intoxicate you with the illusion that they are
MORE THAN -
when they, like you, are simply a sum of their parts
pieces of their past & broken hearts
a painful end to what was a beautiful start

Communication lost in accusations
He told me to never stop choosing him but he never seemed
to choose me
confused in his misconception of me
that he actually thinks I needed him to be happy
they say people search for fault in others to hide their own
insecurities
     failing to see,
that there is actually strength in vulnerability

Pain is what made me; heartbreak is what completed me
I grew from the emptiness that surrounded me
     wanting love is *not* needy
it's knowing you need sun to blossom beautifully
there is nothing more pure than to love naturally, deeply

How can an attraction run so deep
emotion floods my sleep
     like poetry I'm in it knee deep
no effort - no reciprocity
connected but no connection

circles is the only direction
yet a circle is completion
so why are we not complete?

That morning he came at me; so cold
it felt like he was fighting for control
his words an attempt to dim my light
did he think that would make him shine?
that it would make the darkness of his mistakes disappear
if he pointed his finger at mine?

I know I've told him I DON'T NEED HIM
I simply *wanted* him
was that not enough - or was it just too much?
now that it's just him...and just I
was there ever an us?
years later and left with nothing but my own heart

a painful end to what was a beautiful start

SHALLOW WATERS

She read him like a book yet he always read her wrong
thinking he could rewrite her instead
actions he would later regret
he searched for the words to piece her together
yet, she had *never* come undone

She fell for who he could have been
an attraction intense
but he had a wavering conscious; always on the defense
lived as if choices didn't come with consequence

If only we could see the future; simply foreshadow
the fact that
you can't expect to find depth when the water is so shallow

She had the strength of a wave but he feared the tide
always trying to tame her; to subtly subside
he tried to force her to stay ashore
the calm before the storm

can't tame what is meant to run free
she was forgiveness without apology
she had a depth that would forever be a mystery
& his intentions were always so contradictory

he never truly saw her value
always fearing he would get lost in her shadow

you'll never find depth in shallow water.

NAIVETY

Suspicion crept in
left to read between the lines of
messages you forgot to delete
lies and deceit
in everything you didn't say
you carefully chose what to portray

Shoulda known simply by
the way she looked at me
that it was more between you
than just some history
the look on her face gave me answers
to questions I didn't even know I had
to ask

if you tell the truth then you don't have to remember
at the time you didn't know I had seen you with her
disappointed that you turned out to be
every bit of a lie, unmistakably
didn't want to believe I could be so naïve
blind to what was now
right in front of me

SHAME ON YOU

Wondered if I should ask you where you were last night

just so you could deny it
take the truth & rewrite it

Beware, if a woman is asking you certain questions
it's 'cause she already knows the answer
thought you knew me better
to underestimate my intuition

realized it was a reasonable suspicion
when I saw your car
was parked outside her house this morning

disappointed & hurt
cringed when I saw her
all I could think was wow, you could actually do better
but now that I think of it, she should do better
because while I was in the dark
she's playing her part
to a man who has no regard
for the value of a woman's heart

NO INTEGRITY

Shoulda known when the only thing consistent was
inconsistency

6 am exposing reality
message on the screen proving your dishonesty
my mistake for believing you had moral integrity

the disappointment runs deep
deeper than your lies
deeper than your truth

shattered intimacy
guess it explains the hesitancy

wasted time
artificially refined

suffering from emotional disconnect
lost yourself in the casualties of sex

never got the rules to the games you played
funny how silence can manipulate
so let me just reiterate -

I'm not mad; you simply lost my respect
guess I thought more of you than you ever thought of
yourself

WTF

I don't get it
I don't get you

There's no romance in an emoji
No foreplay in a text
So let me get this right –
You left
Just to come *right* back?

Sittin' here shakin' my head
Sex deeper than our recent conversations
Then I gotta listen
to how you despise confrontation
let's face it, you just struggle with communication!

Guess I'm not supposed to pull your card
Or blow up your spot, right?
But baby, I don't bite my tongue for anyone

So simple
You makin' it hard
If you not gonna let me in your head
Guess you can stay the hell outta my bed
Harsh, nah,
Just real

You don't know what you want
Can't say what you feel

Stop wastin' my time
If this is a game, guess I don't know the rules
If fact, forget it,
I've never been one to follow the rules –

Mixed signals, mixed messages
Too many games
Stay, go
Damn sure learned
Not everyone's who they *POST* to be
Not who I thought you'd turn out to be

But I ain't gonna blame you,
    I blame me
Shoulda been able to see
Shit ain't that deep
Nothin' left for me
Walking away,
I give up

Yet, I'm still sittin' here like *what the fuck...*

COMPLICATIONS

Fear and the lack of flexibility
Selfishness and insecurity
I don't need you to fulfill me
Because I am NOT empty

Love isn't dependency
Yet you define it as attachment
Turning conversation into an argument
Communication into complications

Manipulating my words
to create your own meaning
Unable to express what you're feeling

As I ask questions
You accuse me of making assumptions
Clearly you don't know me

Truthfully,
I'm not sure you even know yourself.

GEMINI

Double vision
Astrological prediction
An angel in disguise
Watch the darkness rise
Mind contaminated with misconceptions and lies
Two sides like a Gemini
Overcome with jealousy
All over a mutual discrepancy
I see the way you look at me
Like I've suddenly become the enemy
Insensitive
Actions always contradictory
Momentary stability
Intrigued with the novelty of my attention
Forgetting it's merely a conversation
Then wanna call me a tease
'Cause I can hang with all men and still have 'em respect me
Dangerous flirtations
Simple fornications
A smile charming only to a serpent
Unsavory acts in need to repent
It's yet another confirmation
Of your loyalty
And how it's only to yourself

RUMORS

Never been one to hide shit
    It is what it is
Assumptions spoken in quiet whispers

Did he hit me?
Did I cheat?
Because apparently I was seen with so & so…
& then they talk about how *he ain't no good;*
how could I not know…
Did he get caught lying?
Did he leave me crying?
They heard I was three months along
They know we been fighting; raised voices…
And so & so said we were weighing our choices…
Then two days later the story always changes…

Small minds discuss people
they belittle; nothing viable
Gossip makes your reality unstable
You're speaking about business that was
never yours
Turning unnamed battles into world wars

All these rumors; nothing but small talk
I was never concerned
Just another lesson learned
It's nothing for me to walk out

Guess that will leave ya'll with more to talk about.

HESITATION

Curiosity led to infatuation
From the initial conversation
Interest-undeniable
Yet…there was mutual hesitation

Hearts previously broken
{Guarded}
In inability to trust
In ourselves, in us

Weeks turned into months
Making it that much harder
To avoid the passion in your kiss
Neither of us expecting this
Suddenly, your arms began to feel safe
Our own private place

Hands intertwined
We understood all the things
we couldn't find the words to say
wouldn't say
we had fallen many times
in these moments; yours & mine

In fear of letting you in – I'd push you away

BUT still you stayed
A friendship – a bond
Unbreakable, undeniable

Infatuation had brought us closer to love; an understanding

YET....there was mutual hesitation
Hearts previously broken
{Guarded}

Words once unspoken, now heard
Felt
I trusted you, you trusted me
Or so I thought

If love is blind then how could we see
That what we needed was what we wanted
Hands intertwined; yours & mine

Still we couldn't find a way
Time after time
Letting others cloud our mind
Frustration heightened, intoxicated arguments
Fearing what our hearts felt

We fooled ourselves into thinking we tried

We hide behind pride

In silence I walked out
In hesitation & in doubt

LOST MEN; EASILY CONFLICTED

Conflicted
Easily influenced -
Reciting from the book of psalms won't make you a preacher
& herding sheep damn sure don't make you a leader

I'd go deeper but I don't wanna lose you
Confuse you
Expose you
'Cause you always claim to keep it real
But there's nothing original in being artificial

You say you got pride
But you can stand to swallow some of those words before
they become lies

Recognize that negativity evolves too
Insecurity screams even in silence
Allowing flaws to become a weakness
Your ego, an Achilles heel
Your heart, mind and soul concealed
Afraid to reveal, afraid to heal

Potential is pointless without effort
Like a question that goes unanswered
There may be purpose in being a Shepard
but not when your destined to be king
There's no refund on unfilled dreams

When will you realize
Open your eyes, follow your heart
Complacent has become your disguise

The end is nowhere to start
Your swallowing sin in every shot of Remy
Looking for answers in a bottle till it's empty

The streets don't love you
All those sleepless nights can't hold you
Your lyin' to yourself every time you look in the mirror

I ain't tellin' you nothin' you don't need to hear
Avoidance shows fear

Stand up, man up
Envision what your capable of
Turn possibility into actuality
Dreams into reality
Embrace you're fate &
Change the probability

MEN

Men are this, men are that
Dogs, dicks
And doormats -for your own insecurities

Tall dark & handsome
Eyes you can get lost in
But all you see is game

Recycled, recited, memorized
& closets full of skeletons
Rather than the broken hearts they hide
Because they were taught not to cry

A mystery
Kisses sweet but according to you they're rarely meant to be
A fantasy
You aren't interested in their reality

Men
Strong, brave and proud
A smile you want to taste
Whispering
Sweet words of nothing, you hear no substance
Licking their lips, their wounds
No respect for the gift *you* gave up to soon

Men
Liars, cheaters, and heartbreakers

Men
Baby daddies, felons and frauds

Men
Torn down by the women who claim to love them
Discarded the moment they make a mistake

Men
Our Men
Are being thrown behind bars, shot down, profiled and
executed
Unemployed, uneducated, miseducated
   And simply misunderstood

Men
Who were created to love, provide and protect
We emasculated
For the sake of "independence"

It's okay to be frustrated, but feminism
Doesn't mean we are so strong we can't love them
Love is strength

You don't have to "raise no man'
But how 'bout you try to encourage one?
So busy chasing "Mr. Wrong"

So you swear there's no Mr. Right
only concerned with what he can do for you
    tonight
Because Beyoncé told you he was replaceable, you told him
his shit was to the left
    And he left

Now you're bitter and swear you don't need a man
So they treat you as if they aren't needed
Said they don't know how to act, that they ain't a man
But you never bothered to treat him right
You never saw in him…*a man*

Men
Our backbone, a shared rib bone
Our men, our heart….our home
Love him, embrace him, enlighten him
Encourage, support, comfort – elevate

We are stronger together than apart
Un-break his heart

PAST LIVES

WE never speak of feelings
Avoidance personified
WHY?

Dangerous territory
Undefined
Perhaps I've locked the doors
Because occasions
of feelings
of past lives
Left scars in my mind
As you left your life behind
The temptations to experience
Feelings again
get denied
From fear of wound abrasion
Invasion of a past world
    a past life

Similar experiences are knocking
Too close to old familiar doors
If only the past weren't so close
To the surface…
If only we got to say good-bye

DOUBLE SUSPICION

Wounded hearts cry so gracefully
Hiding tears, I hate to let you see

Frustrations CLIMAX

Still we hide behind false masks
Gave you the truth only when you asked

Passing days
Longing for something more

As you turn away
I close the door never asking you to stay
I wonder if you ran to her
& you can't help but wonder
Who is he?
Who was wrong,
you or me?

Tristin Jacy

I CALLED YOUR NAME

You call my name

    I do not listen

As you whisper sweet words of forever

I know not what forever means
A past filled with heart breaks and broken dreams

You call my name

    I do not listen

You reach for my hand
When I leave
You don't understand
You call my name

    I do not listen

You pull me near
With such innocence
Gently you kissed me

You say my name

    I do not listen

You tell me that you love me

    I do not listen

Last night while I lay in bed
You came to tell me what might have been
With tears in your eyes
That I had never noticed; never seen
You said good-bye

I heard you say good-bye

I tried to call your name

    But you did not listen.

HE LOVES ME NOT

He loves me, he loves me not
here today, gone tomorrow
he doesn't lead, but he wants me to follow

He loves me, he loves me not
is there trust or insecurity
all this confidence; hiding jealous tendencies

He loves me, he loves me not
lies or hidden truths
when there's secrecy, how can you ever find real intimacy

He loves me, he loves me not
searching for depth,
but you can't read what's taken out of context

He loves me, he loves me not
like art, I want you to be inspiring
but there's just no wisdom without understanding

He loves me, he loves me not
gone today, gone tomorrow
I left because of a need to be free;
I was never meant to follow

NO HAPPY ENDING

I felt your love every time you touched me
It soothed those wicked lies which cut me

The lies you made to sound so sincere
Unfortunately there is no happy ending here

They say even the devil has a charming side
Intoxicating lust I can't even describe
When it came to you I threw logic aside

Wanted what I knew was wrong
Loved what I had hated for so long

A feeling so intense
I was lost in the confusion
That somehow seemed to all make sense

A PIECE OF ADVICE

Never drown yourself in troubled waters;

you can always tell how conscious a man is -how aware-
if he treats his woman the way he'd want a man to treat his
daughters

Can't tell you how to live your life
just here to offer some advice
the solution should never feel like a sacrifice

I mean here you are with a beautiful soul
becoming a victim to manipulation & control

a reality that's hard to confront
emotions hard to console

There's nothing wrong in sleeping alone
Just like there's nothing wrong
with you ignoring those messages he just sent to your phone

Never let a man disrespect you
lie, cheat or embarrass you
value your self-worth
it's not always selfish to put yourself first

TWELVE WEEKS

This picture; black and white
Is all that is left of life

Can't help but wonder what could have been
Not sure how we got here
Still so hard to comprehend

Decisions are like words
That can't be taken back
We cracked under the pressure
Had different reasons but we both felt trapped
Threats, love, hate, obsession

You lashed out in fear
Too scared to face your own guilty confession
Hidden truths; hidden conception

With bittersweet kisses
You tried to ease the loss
You crawled into bed beside me

But I still felt so empty

A heart beat too weak
to withstand the pain of the world
Too innocent to be touched by you

A pain you'll never be able to erase
No matter how many tears
you wipe from my face

An emptiness
that empty promises simply can't replace

A part of me; a part of you
Became a part of your lies;
But a part of our truth
now part of our past

The life we made
Like us - it wasn't meant to last

LESSONS

When we add up all our wrongs, are we ever bound to get it
right?

they say love is worth the fight
but if it's real it wouldn't leave us with so many sleepless
nights

all these unanswered questions
& unread texts
always on edge tryin' to anticipate what comes next

there's no comfort in the unknown
no forgiveness for the things others condone
There are some things you just know
times you just gotta let go

We aren't always given reasons to understand
why some people are meant to be lessons
while others become blessings

It's not always easy to make sense of what we felt
all we can do is play the cards we are dealt
pay attention to what the stars reveal
and allow our hearts time to heal

WHERE PAIN COMES FROM

It's easy to point fingers
easy to place blame
can't make sense of what's not explained
when feelings are at stake-it's never a game
he blamed her for the pain
he blamed love for making him this way
　　but it was never love that hurt him
it was never her that broke him
pain comes from not being able to forgive
from being stuck on that one perspective
pain comes from holding on when we should simply let go
from withering when we were meant to grow
even when everything comes undone
we have the power to become
the power to resist
looking for answers in a kiss
instead of from within
will only leave you with regrets
when you gonna learn, you can't change anyone else
you can only change yourself.

WILTED FLOWERS

You sent flowers thinking that was an apology
But you were never actually sorry
Never could own your shit
Like it would kill you to admit it
Now the flowers are wilted
Dying
Because you wanted the beauty
But never wanted to help it grow
Like the sincerity you could never show
You loved how I loved you
And you took what I could give you
Selfishly it was always about you
You'll misconstrue any truth and make it untrue
Even when I forgave you,
you wanted to believe
even *that* was about you

LIKE NO OTHER

He says my face is innocent, but my mouths a little slick
Know just how to piss him off – *real quick*
Just another one of our antics
Think we like to fight just so we can make up
Without crossing the line

I'm the reason to his rhyme
{Will even send him a nasty pic from time to time}
Know how to keep him happy; know how to keep it hard
Damn sure drives him crazy

But – I am his consistency
That type that's hard to find
Still learning the depths of his mind

Just wanna be the softness after a hard day
The right direction when he loses his way
Love when he calls just to hear my voice
Love how he loves me like there's no other choice

SPARE ME THE FAIRYTALE

He said "oh you a feisty one"
Guess I wasn't supposed to have an opinion
To him, a closed mouth was more convenient
Except I've always spoken my mind
Handled my own grind
His bitter approach was a waste of my time
Never been the type to be told what to do
Not the girl you can simply subdue
Cause I won't back down
Quiet down
Bow down
Fall down to my knees
To appease his patriarchal ideology
And that doesn't mean I don't honor femininity
I just want my own voice & individuality
Some days I'm feisty
Others I may be angry
Then turn around and want to be loved
Held tight, hugged and told everything will be alright
Some days I need space, the freedom to be ME
Can't get lost in becoming a "We"
Spare me the fairytale cause I don't need to be saved

CHECK MATE

Conceptual manifestation
Verbal exploitation
Mental analyzation
What's real to you?

Fantasy
Complexity
    Or are your thoughts too elementary
    Wanting to read deep into simplicity
    But can't grasp anything intellectually

Your existence mediocre
Rational inferior
Spiritually a prisoner
    Of adverse conformity

I will *never* be what you want
Nor expect me to be

If a response isn't what you were looking for
Then don't come for me

My verbal ability
Is a living entity

In whose meaning you can explore
Never findin' what you're lookin' for
    I hide, disguise
    The soul that lies behind my eyes

I can wrap it in truth
Decorate it in lies
    What's the difference
    Neither will make you wise

Perceptions become reality
So it's reality that lies
When you're in search of the truth
It's the truth that hides

Foolishly masqueraded
Forming the thoughts in your mind
In which I've just invaded
    Your next move, blockaded

So you thought you knew me
Perception so deceiving
Reality simply misleading
    An ego blinds
The pleasure a heart can find

Selfishness destroys even the hands of time
Victimized by fragile pride
Principles become undignified

Lacking the introspect
To rationalize

Too unaware to visualize
Your future's moving
Counterclockwise

So quick to speculate
Allow me to formally denunciate

Playing to eradicate

Checkmate.

DEEP ENOUGH TO DROWN

Like the warmth of a fire
If you get too close you'll get burned
You can make love to me
Doesn't mean you won't get hurt

Don't fantasize about me
When you haven't taken the time to undress my soul
Touching my skin doesn't mean you know
Anything about me

    Physical ecstasy
    Mental intimacy
And you're *still* stuck on tryin' to seduce me
On nothing more than simple chemistry

Please don't get too attached
By no means is this some perfect match
When it's done there's no going back
Where's the reality in a fairytale romance?

The water will take your breath, leave you spellbound

Even in shallow water it's still deep enough to drown

THREE BROKEN DEFINITIONS

Truth:
Is nothing but honesty
Merely an agreement with reality
But you chose to deceive, mislead
And it was my fault to believe

Respect:
Why is it so hard for you to treat me
As I deserve to be
As if you have never heard of
Equality; reciprocity

Commitment:
That's what the words *"I trust you"* meant
Maybe if I would have opened my eyes –
I would've been able to see
Faithful was something you were never gonna be

Did you ever feel my heart break…
As you forgot to give
But continued to take

YOU WILL LOVE AGAIN

Heartbreak never brings pleasure
Through the tears you can find gratitude
Honor your reflection; a single feather
to give thanks for the lessons bestowed
In the end, karma is all that we are actually owed
Find peace within

You will love again

With growth comes pain
A flower can't blossom without the right amount of rain
Let the water strengthen you
Clean the wounds; let it heal you
Find strength within

You will love again

Every end becomes a new beginning
Sometimes letting go is just as befitting
Find beauty even in the flaws
Embrace only positive thoughts
Find happiness within

You will love again

A Love Letter to the Man who Never Loved Me,

I want you to know I loved you. From the moment our eyes first met there was an attraction that grew over the years into something neither of us expected. I fell for your passion, your intensity and your optimism. All the sweet words and affection that you showered me with, made it hard not to fall right into your arms. You had a way of making me feel desired, I felt it in the way you looked at me, how you would move the hair out of my face before kissing me and the way you pulled me closer into you every time you held me. Each time we made love it was more passionate than the last. I wanted you, at times even craved you, and you were so deep beneath my skin it was hard to imagine ever being intimate with anyone else.

What we had was complicated. It was an intoxicating infatuation, a slight obsession, a friendship that caught fire and left us with the burns to prove it. I thought I knew you. I thought I knew the dark parts of your past, the empty space of your heart and the secrets of your soul. I thought I loved you, even the parts you couldn't love about yourself. I thought I understood your weaknesses, your faults. I accepted them.

Years and years, of laughter and of pain. Memories; some perfect and some painful. Endless days and nights of conversation, kisses, of moments shared. A bond that seemed unbreakable. You stood by me through every bad day and bad mood, never forgetting to tell me I was beautiful. Every time we made love it was like you couldn't get enough of me.

Yet, I am not sure you ever really loved me, although I am sure you believed you did. You simply loved how I loved you. You loved what I could give you; the encouragement and support. You loved how it fed your ego. You loved the passion, the adventure and the laughter. But love isn't selfish and you took more than you ever gave. Love is about truth and acceptance and for years, you fabricated a life that was built on lie after lie. Love doesn't create insecurities and we all know you always questioned my loyalty only because you *knew* you were guilty of everything you accused me of doing. You feared me finding out the truth and leaving. You feared me finding the love I deserved. I read somewhere once, to never underestimate a man's power to make you feel guilty for his mistakes and that, my love, was something you had mastered early. Remember the first time you told me you loved me? Do you remember how I didn't say it back? Maybe subconsciously it's because I knew, it wasn't real - it wasn't true.

Yet, I don't regret loving you. It was genuine, it was real and it was everything I had to give. People come into your life for a reason, and while I am still recovering from you, and still trying to understand my own lesson, I would like to believe I showed you what real love has to offer. I hope I showed you the love you seem incapable of giving right now so that perhaps one day you can grow from this.

Hopefully one day you will be a better man that you ever

were to me. Maybe one day you will understand the value of honesty. I hope I gave you love when you needed it the most. You were a lesson, I will always hold close.

In love and forgiveness,

Yours Truly

a single feather
to give thanks for the lessons bestowed

~ *Tristin Jacy*

ABOUT THE AUTHOR

Tristin Jacy is a Native American poet from Buffalo, New York. She has taught writing for over ten years at Buffalo State College and is the mother of two children.

www.ingramcontent.com/pod-product-compliance
Lightning Source LLC
Chambersburg PA
CBHW071100090426
42737CB00013B/2410